Living Life Fully with
Macular Degeneration

Living Life Fully with Macular Degeneration

Doris Winn Polak

LIVING LIFE FULLY WITH MACULAR DEGENERATION

iUniverse books may be ordered through booksellers or by contacting:

iUniverse
1663 Liberty Drive
Bloomington, IN 47403
www.iuniverse.com
844-349-9409

ISBN: 978-1-6632-1149-1 (sc)
ISBN: 978-1-6632-1150-7 (e)

Library of Congress Control Number: 2020920546

Print information available on the last page.

iUniverse rev. date: 11/06/2020

This book is dedicated to the memory of my mother.
Irene Hargis Winn
1908-1993

CONTENTS

PREFACE

I have pretty eyes, or at least that is what many people through the years have told me. Blue eyes and red hair is a rather nice combination. Yes, my eyes are pretty, but they do not work well.

This point was spotlighted for me a few years ago when my eye doctor told me that

I had developed macular degeneration.

The macula is only a bit larger than a grain of rice. How could something so small cause so much trouble to so many people? Right now there are more than 10 million people in the United States who have this debilitating disease, and there are more than 200 million in the world with it.

What does the macula do, anyway?

Actually, it's one of the most important parts of the eye because it gives us our central vision. The macula lets us read. It allows us to watch television. We recognize our grandchild's face by using our macula; we order off the menu using it. When it doesn't work, or if it works poorly, we have to give up our cars and possibly lose our independence, and worse yet, it could keep us from living in our own home. A degenerating macula is not a good thing!

I didn't know much about the disease then, but now I feel that I am almost an expert. If you are newly diagnosed and would like to understand what you and your eyes can expect over the next weeks, months and years, pour yourself some coffee, pull up a chair, and get started reading my story.

Through intellectualizing this disease, I want you to be able to live your life to the fullest while having macular degeneration.

ACKNOWLEDGEMENTS

A special thanks to my editor and dearest friend, John C. Huber.

HOW IT ALL BEGAN

On June 13, 1991, my life took quite a turn for the worse. Probably because of those pretty blue eyes and red hair, I was predisposed to getting skin cancer. So, on that fateful day, the doctor said that I had nodular melanoma and had a 5% chance to live. After several surgeries, a good dosing of chemotherapy and many other drugs, I was starting to feel better and began to enjoy some books that a friend had brought me. As I reached for one of the books, I dropped my glasses, shattering both lenses. The optometrist was able to see me that day, but she said that because my prescription was out of date, I would have to have an examination.

She looked into my right eye and said everything looked

great. But when she examined the left eye, she said, 'Oh, you have a large nevus or freckle next to the optic nerve."

She went on to explain that this was certainly not a rare finding, but because of the subcutaneous melanoma that had just a few weeks before been removed from my shoulder, we should watch the "spot" for a while.

I casually mentioned this to my surgeon and oncologist,

and the next thing I knew, I was going getting CAT scans and MRIs. The final opinion was to watch it carefully, and I was sent to an ophthalmologist who did just that.

Now fast forward to 2014 at an appointment with a Retina Specialist in Indianapolis where I had moved. After we discussed the state of my nevus, He told me that he saw changes in the epithelial cells in the back of my eye. Since he was a man of few words, I waited until I got to my regular eye doctor, a fine ophthalmologist in whom I had the highest regard and trust. I knew he could and would fill in the blanks for me. He explained the changes in one succinct sentence. "You have ARMD, AGE RELATED MACULAR DEGENERATION."

Looking back, I do not know why I was so shocked. After all, my mother had the disease and was blind in one eye, and had really poor vision in the other when she died at the age of eighty-five. I knew that the disease was familial, so why wasn't I prepared?

I recall peppering the poor doctor with question after question, some of which he had answers for and some he did not. Many questions regarding macular degeneration have no answers. He was kind and compassionate yet did not paint a particularly rosy picture for me.

Luckily, my son Jonathan had attended the appointment with me, and after we left the office, we talked about the implications for me, and we decided that it was a wait-and-see situation. We would handle problems as they occurred.

It is not the purpose of this book to give medical information about the disease itself. You can look that up online and delve into it as deeply as you would like. But here is a quick synopsis. That day, the doctor explained to me that there are two kinds of ARMD, wet and dry. Most people, like I was that day, are faced with dry, and then about 10% of them will change to wet. The disease itself causes an erratic growth of blood vessels in the back of the eye. When those poorly formed vessels start to leak, that is known as wet macular degeneration. It is dangerous because if the leaking fluid is left unchecked, it will cause scarring, and that will result in loss of vision.

He went on to explain that if mine would turn to wet RMD, I would be given regular injections to reduce the chance of the erratic growth of vessels.

"That's what you think, Doc," I thought to myself. "There is never going be a time I will have a shot in my eyeball. Never!"

For several months, all was well. At the appointments, the staff carefully took pictures of my retina, macula, and fundus, and upon examination, the doctor would say I was doing well. But one time, he said something else.

The doctor's words stunned me. "Things have changed; you now have wet MD. It is time to start the injections."

"Well, I will think about it and will let you know when I come back next month what I would like to do." I tried to act and sound nonchalant about the possibility.

He said, "I don't think you understand. We need to start the injections today. Right now!"

I considered my possibilities. I was way too old to jump up out of the chair and run home; my son had driven me to the appointment, and I was at a high risk of embarrassing him. They were both staring at me and waiting for me to act like a grownup. After all, I was seventy-four years old. I muttered something, and before I knew it, the procedure was finished and I was on my way home.

At this writing, I have had nearly seventy shots, but none of them were as scary is that first one. Now I get two injections each time since I have developed a sensitivity to the previously used topical numbing agent. So now I get an injection of a Novocain-like medication that numbs the eyeball. After a few minutes, the doctor reappears in the room and does the second injection.

I have learned how to deal with the injections, and although it's not a picnic, it's not the end of the world either.

I go to the appointment and get the shots, come home and rest, and usually by later that evening, all is well.

Here are some injection tips:

- Remember that the doctor does not want you to be uncomfortable. Speak up. Ask for more numbing drops. Ask to wait a moment until you can get your breath and calm yourself down. Be in control.

- Be aware what drops are going into your eye. I always ask the nurse what drug she's using if she doesn't tell me in advance. I have developed a sensitivity or allergy to several eye medications, so I always ask. I would rather seem a little pushy than be up all night with a post-injection problem.

- Before you leave the office, make sure that you have asked the doctor what you can use for pain afterward if needed. For instance, I usually continue flushing my eye with lubricant over-the-counter eye drops. My doctor advised me that I could use the single-use vial of the product as often as every ten minutes if needed. I also use either a warm or cool damp compress on the eye for the first few hours when I get home.

And I always take an Advil and get comfy on the couch for an hour or so.

You must know, however, that many people have no pain involved with the shot at all. A few have told me that they go back to work following the appointment. I guess it's an individual thing, so you have to do what is best for you.

A few times after the shot, the eyeball gets a blood spot. That can be quite disconcerting when it happens the first time. All it means is that you have a bruise in your eye which will go away in a few days. It doesn't hurt at all, but the eyeball may look quite angry.

One problem that I had was soon after I moved to Texas. I got the injection on a Friday and then did my usual routine of Advil, rest, lubricating drops, and of course, a wet compress. By Friday evening, my eye was really hurting, and I couldn't seem to get it to calm down. Water was running down my face from the eye constantly. Saturday morning was much the same, a drippy and painful eye. By Sunday morning I still saw no improvement, so I knew I was going to have to get some help. I was so relieved when I called the practice, and they told me that my doctor was on call. She called me back quickly, and after I described the problem to her, she said that she needed to see me. She was just finishing up an emergency surgery and would wait for me in her downtown office. I called my fabulous daughter, Vanessa, who lives seven minutes from me, and soon we were on our way in hopes of getting some relief.

Dr. Ghafoori examined the eye carefully and saw that the point of the injection looked good, and she was wondering what could be the problem. Then she decided to roll over the top eyelid up and look underneath – – and there it was, a tiny fiber from the washcloth that I had been using as the moist compress. Once she removed it, my eye stopped tearing, and I stopped complaining. Vanessa and I even stopped for ice cream on the way home. The lesson that I learned is that when something doesn't feel right, investigate and get help.

Another strange problem cropped up right about the time I was starting to get the monthly injections. One day I was walking back from the park with my Shih Tzu and was nearly home. I looked toward the street and there was a sleek, large racing car being pushed by three men. Now I lived in a lovely suburban area, and even though it was a few minutes from Indianapolis, I had never seen a race car on any street, much less on mine. It was approaching me slowly and when I stopped, so did it. I blinked my eyes a few times, and the car and men were gone. I looked at the situation again and realized that what I thought was the black car was actually my black mailbox.

The men pushing the car were branches only a few inches from my eyes.

I had read about the Charles Bonnet Syndrome, yet I was mystified that it had actually happened to me. When I told my eye doctor about my racing car hallucination, he explained that in the mid-1700s, a man named Charles Bonnet noticed that people who were otherwise coherent and of a good mental stature would start having hallucinations as they lost their vision. The brain apparently gets a garbled message from the eyes and tries to make sense of it but fails. It is not a rare occurrence. It kept me entertained nicely for several months, and then it just stopped.

So now I had a new label, wet macular degeneration. Actually, it's called wet age-related macular degeneration, but I refuse I to say the AGE part. Is that being vain?

I asked the doctor what else I could do to help myself besides getting a shot once a month. He recommended AREMD2 vitamins which are available at many grocery stores, Target, plus Sam's and Costco. They are not expensive and are said by research to help.

The other positive thing the doctor said I could do was eat lots of kale and spinach.

The deeper green the color of the vegetable, the higher value the food is for your eyes. So, I began buying and eating kale. At first, I didn't care for it, but I persisted and developed a taste for it raw in my salad, and I also found that it was delicious steamed. I went to Pinterest online and experimented with the many different kale recipes there.

Things went pretty smoothly for me for several months. I

had a few emergencies along the way, mostly when my doctor was out of the country on vacation with his family. After the second time that happened, I suggested to him to ask his wife and kids if they minded me going on their trips with them. Actually, I was left in good hands while he was gone, and I made it through each problem that came along.

For many people, and perhaps most people, the

disease is slow-moving. In fact, some patients get diagnosed, and it progresses so slowly that it is never a problem. Unfortunately for me, that was not the case.

One morning I woke up and my right eye was just fine, but by noon I was noticing a major change in it. Everything was turning gray and indistinct. I called the doctor's office and was told that... yes, you guessed it, he was on vacation.

I knew I should've gone with them!

The office receptionist was so helpful, though, and she made arrangements for me to get seen by another ophthalmologist almost immediately. That doctor examined me for a long time and then sent me to a Retina Specialist who sent me to a specialist in Chicago a few days later. By the time I got to see that doctor, I could see little out of my right eye. He told me that the disease is supposed to be slow-moving, but my eye had not followed the disease protocol. I now had only one workable eye.

A few months later, I made the decision to leave the Midwest and return to Texas. I would be leaving my beloved son and his family, supportive friends, and my ophthalmologist. I was truly off on a new adventure.

CHOOSING YOUR DOCTOR

You and your doctor are going to be forming a partnership to care for your diseased eye or eyes, so you need to do some work to find just the right match.

When I moved to the Indianapolis area, I decided to join a church choir. It was a large congregation, and the choir was and still is excellent. I needed to find an eye doctor. I was standing outside the choir rehearsal room having a conversation with a couple of altos about who they would recommend. Funny thing, in unison they both said the same name. I asked them how to spell the name, and a third voice popped up, another choir member who was just walking by and overheard what we were saying. "I can tell you how to spell the name. "B E H F O R O U Z," she said emphatically. "I was his office manager for a long time, and I can tell you he is one fine ophthalmologist. His patients are so impressed with his problem-solving ability. That did it. The next day I made an appointment and found Dr. Behforouz living up to all the fine comments and kudos others had given him. Eighteen months later when I told him that I was moving to Texas, he offered to help me find someone there who could help me. He did some research, and so did I. I went to the private Facebook page for macular degeneration patients and asked the question who could recommend a good practice in the Austin area. Even though the message board is global in scope, I got an immediate reply with a great well-thought of practice about twenty minutes from the place where I would be living.

I carefully researched each of the eight doctors in the Austin practice, all of whom were retina specialists. Fortunately, there was a bio for each showing where they had gone to school, where they had spent their time doing fellowships, etc. I took that information with me to my last appointment with

Dr. B., and we discussed the pros and cons of each doctor on the list. I then asked him to make the final decision for me, and I could not be more delighted with his choice. Dr. Shelley Day Ghafoori, my new doctor, now is truly a partner in my eye care. She is kind, thoughtful and thorough. I trust her to make intelligent decisions on my behalf. And perhaps most of all, she is approachable and conversant about any problems or any concerns that I have. I have now seen her approximately every twenty-eight days for nearly three years. My respect for her and the staff in her office is profound.

Choosing your doctor is really important. Sometimes you may not be in tune with each other. When that happened to me in another medical area, I have left the practice and looked for someone more likely to help me. If you live in a smaller town and don't have many options, you might need to have a conversation with the doctor and see if you can work out any issues that you feel uncomfortable with. Shop around; get second opinions when you need to.

In addition to my RS, I also have had wonderful success seeing a Low Vision Specialist, Dr. Miller, recommended to me by my primary eye doctor. I know that this is not true, but it seems like for every problem I present her with, she says 'Oh, let's see if this device will clear that up for you." Whether it is her sunny disposition and can-do attitude or the array of lamps, lights, magnifiers and a multitude of other gadgets and devices she has, I always walk out of an appointment with her feeling like a million dollars.

Let me give you some

examples of how she has helped me. She asked me what I like to do in my spare time. I remarked that one of the things my friend and I like the most is attending performances by Ballet Austin and the Austin Symphony. We go out for a lovely dinner, then go to the performance, and we really enjoy the evening.

"Can you actually see the performers on the stage?" she asked.

"No," I said softly.

"Let me try to help you with that." She showed me a monocular that I could use with my one working eye, and it made my evening at the ballet so vibrant. I could see the costumes. I could see the expressions on the dancers' faces and the leg, foot, arm and even finger positions. I could SEE! The monocular comes in various strengths, and I only have one strength left higher than what I am using now. I have no doubt that Dr. Miller will be able to help me with something else when I outgrow this device.

I have tried do use the monocular at home with subtitles on the television. It has not worked well for me, but I will persist until I can master it.

I have also purchased my favorite piece of equipment from her. It is a large magnifier called ONYX HD by Freedom Scientific. When it was delivered to me, I had it set up in the kitchen on my bar, and now eighteen months later, it is still there. Absolutely, it is my lifeline. I keep it in the kitchen area because I use it to see medications and their dosage, to read my recipes, to read my mail, and for a myriad other tasks. Not only will it highly magnify what I am reading, but it also will read aloud to me what is on the screen. Another feature that it has is changing the color of either the text or the background. I would just be lost without it.

If you live in a smaller town without a low vision specialist accessible to you, look online and get catalogs so you can order these and other devices.

ORGANIZATION

Perhaps the most important concept you can foster in your life is being organized. I suppose this is important if you have good sight or if you were like I am, using one not-so good eye. Let's look at some situations in your home and in your life that will help you get and stay organized. It did not take me long to learn that I needed to put things in certain places and in certain orders to keep from having problems. I like to cook, and the kitchen was the first place that I had problems. One day I decided to make some Snickerdoodle cookies which are basically a sugar cookie with a good amount of cinnamon on them. I had the cookie dough almost completed except for the cinnamon. I picked up the container and just before I shook it into the dough, for some reason, I held it to my nose and took a whiff of my favorite spice, cinnamon. Only it wasn't. It was cumin, which I use when making Mexican food. I love it, but not in my snickerdoodles.

I decided that I needed to rearrange my four-tier spice rack. I also made a commitment to myself to always put each spice back where it came from. I was just going to have to memorize where things were – savory spices on the rack at the top, sweet spices like my precious cinnamon on the second rack, bottles of vanilla and other extracts and dyes on the third rack, and an assortment of other things on the bottom. Easily done, and disasters of the future averted.

Later I received as a gift, a PENfriend2. The box contained self-adhesive labels on which you can record your voice to say "Thyme," or "Sage," or "Cinnamon." Then you touch the label with the pen and you will hear your voice say the name of the spice. Pretty nifty. And you can use it on CD labels, files or a plethora of other places. It is important not only to be organized but to be safe in the kitchen. Storage of knives and other sharp objects need to be put in a special place each and every time that they are used. Also be careful when you put knives in the dishwasher. Always put them in a way that when you reach in and can't see them, they will not cut you.

I suppose there's nothing much in the refrigerator that you can get hurt with, but it sure is aggravating when you don't see well to open the door of the refrigerator and stand there looking and looking – – and looking for something. I make it a habit to always put items in the exact same spot. I actually do know where every item is at any time.

Another room where organization skills are so important is the bathroom, and especially the area where makeup is kept. Before I had vision problems, I didn't think twice about how the items of makeup were arranged. After putting body lotion on my hair because I thought it was cream rinse or several other like mishaps, I realized that I needed to really organize the bathroom area.

Ashamedly, I do have a lot of makeup, some I don't use every day. So, I take a brightly colored plastic-lined and zippered bag, and in that I put the five or six items of makeup that I use every day – – cleanser, toner, sunscreen/foundation, eye and lip color. I only use Trinny London makeup which is so easily applied. It goes on the makeup shelf, and because it is bright colored, I can see the bag easily and grab it to use each morning.

On the shelf in the closet, I also keep all my hair products which are clustered together on the left-hand side of the shelf. From there, I put some masks that I don't use often, some nail products that I use even less. Next comes body lotions, followed by perfumes and body sprays. Yikes, that sounds like a lot, doesn't it? But those things mean a lot to me and I like using them.

If you are a newbie to macular degeneration and think like I did—I will read about this, but this will never happen to me— I do hope that you are right and that it does not happen to you, but for me in too short of a time, it became an actuality. Several people have asked me how I can use make up when I no longer can see my face in the mirror. I won't lie, it is a problem. But I always laugh and tell them that my lips, cheeks and eyes have not moved. They are right where they have always been, so I do the best that I can. I live alone, but I have a lot of good friends who when we are together will tell me when I have made a hot mess of things on my face, and I do not mind a bit. I do have a magnifying mirror that

I use to apply my eye makeup, and I'm thankful that I can still see to do that. I try not to use mascara for a week before and a week following an injection.

Medications are another area where you need to be highly organized. Have a headache? Can you find the OTC remedy right away? Cut yourself? You need a Band-Aid. So, I keep my medications in one of the kitchen cabinets. A weekly pill container is on the work area, so I am reminded to take the four prescription drugs daily. I keep the refills and a few other drugs in a cabinet by the refrigerator. The pills themselves are problematic. They are so small that I can't see them to identify what they are after they are out of the container. That means I have to go by feel or color. I was doing fine until one drug company changed a drug which now looked exactly like another medication that I take. I was flummoxed until I felt the new pill; it was rough, and the first pill was really smooth. Hallelujah! No more confusion. I had two healthy eyes on my fingertips!

Here in the Austin area, I live in a 55+ apartment complex. I am so lucky that in both of my bedrooms I have a walk-in closet, so I have plenty of room for my clothes. In the second bedroom closet, I keep clothes for cooler weather like coats, jackets and sweaters. Everything else goes in the big master closet where I have arranged my long sleeve tops, short sleeve tops, pants—black on the right, white in the middle, and navy or patterned on the left. This allows me to find my navy pants and not get them mixed up with the black ones. Also, many times when I am shopping for new clothing, I buy jewelry to complement the outfit; I store everything on one hanger so it is all together in one place.

As far as organization goes, these are only suggestions that work for me. Find your own tips and techniques and be consistent. It will cut down on stress in your life.

SAFETY

Besides being organized, you really need to concern yourself with being safe in every aspect of your daily life. Certainly, a major concern is keeping yourself safe from falling. Here are some tips: I try to intellectualize every step that I take. Is there a curb? Is there moisture or ice around me? Is there a handrail that I could hold onto? Am I close to a turning lane where I could be knocked over by a car? Are there bicycles sharing my space? The possibilities are endless. And I must say, the only time I have fallen down since I was diagnosed really had nothing to do with my eyes. I was in the clubhouse of our complex awaiting to participate in an exercise class that was about to begin. I decided to dash over to the water fountain first. That was fine, but I was not paying attention at all. In fact, I had my head turned towards the side and back, and I was talking a mile a minute to someone behind me. I tripped over a little strip that was separating one room from the next; suddenly I was airborne. I did a tripod landing – – on my temple and my two knees, one of which was a total knee replacement only a few months old. Fortunately, CAT scans and x-rays showed that nothing was broken or damaged, but I did learn a lesson. Think about what you are doing. Pay attention. I have known several people who have had severe falls in their homes because they moved something and later fell over it, or because they lost their balance or for a variety of other reasons. A friend the other day told me that someone in his family had taken a bad fall. She was carrying in groceries. She set some items down on the floor, and when she brought in the next bag of groceries forgot what she had done and down she went. Fortunately, she broke her nose instead of a hip.

Also be careful about throw rugs. If you do not use a tacky strip to anchor them down, the edge can roll up and trip you. The bathroom can be highly dangerous place if you have low vision, and with all the hard surfaces in there, a fall in that room can be deadly. Be sure to install grab bars in the tub and shower BEFORE YOU THINK YOU WILL NEED THEM.

Fernando Pastran, my wonderful friend and personal trainer in Indianapolis worked with me to improve my balance. He had specific exercises which strengthened my core while improving my posture and balance. I am still so grateful for his help and guidance.

WE NEED TO TALK

I love cars. I love how beautiful they are. I love how sleek they are. And I would bottle the new car smell and wear it as perfume if I could. I have bought cars, leased them, rented them. But there comes a time when you need to say, "I am no longer a safe driver." Those seven words should override any thoughts that you have to continue putting yourself and others in harm's way.

A few years ago, when the lease on my nice sedan was coming up for renewal, I decided that I was far too young at seventy-five or so to drive such a dated vehicle. I needed something sharp and jazzy. I needed a red Mustang! I called a dealer close by and told him that I was coming over and was only interested in a red

Mustang with automatic drive. When I got to the dealership, the kind young man had stopped laughing at my phone conversation with him. First of all, nobody wants a car like a Mustang that has automatic drive. That takes away from the total experience, he told me. Not a problem. When I learned to drive, there were no cars except the ones with all the gear shifting. Where was my red car? Why does he show me a black Mustang? He must have been reading my mind because he told me that the red Mustangs are special ordered, and if one does happen to come into the dealership, it's gone in a heartbeat. OK. No problem. A Mustang is a Mustang. He opened the door for me to get in the driver's side. I am not a huge person, but when I saw how tiny the space was, and how low to the ground it was,

I wondered how I would get in or more importantly, if I would ever be able to get out.

I persisted, and wiggled right into the seat. I was ready to go. The salesman looked at me and said, "Can you see out the back window?"

Actually, I could not see anything. I just looked at the salesman and finally shook my head. "I am sorry," he finally said, "In all good conscience I cannot sell you this vehicle.

You would get killed the first time you took it out."

And that was the end of my Mustang Dream. I didn't even get to start the engine. I was defeated by Old Age. I got on my phone and called the salesperson who had leased me my last car and alerted him that I was on my way to his dealership. He helped me to choose a wonderful sedate sedan, and it had all of the safety bells and whistles on it, plus it had a terrific sound system. I was old and yet happy. The Mustang salesman's words haunted me later, though. "Can you see out the back window?" No, and within a few months, I would not be able to see well enough to drive, much less see out the back window.

Should you wait for your doctor or a member of your family to tell you it's time to give up your keys? To "have the talk"? I suppose every person is different, but for me, I definitely knew when it was time to put an end to my love affair with my car. In fact, my son told me to bring the car back to the dealership, and he would meet me there and bring me home. It was a foggy, misty Midwest morning, and I had one heck of a time getting to the dealership that was only thirty minutes away. When I got home, I went into the double garage several times just to look at how empty it was. I had lost my wheels. I had lost my independence.

Or had I? I started to think of all the ways that I could get transportation, and I realized that I would be just fine. I had Lyft and Uber just a click away on my smart phone. I looked into our community services that were available to give rides. Many friends were so generous with their offers to take me to the store, take me to choir rehearsal, take me to the mall. I was going to survive. I was going to be just fine.

And when I put pen to paper, I was coming out ahead of the game financially. With a car payment, insurance, upkeep of the car and gas, taking a shared ride service was much cheaper. And, I was safe, and so were other people on the road.

Be proactive. Don't wait until

something bad happens and then examine the situation by way of your old friend, Hindsight. And don't wait for a family member for the doctor to say, "We need to talk…"

ACTIVITY

Even though your intention is to be safe at all times, you can't just stay in your house. You need exercise and sun to be healthy. My choice in this regard is walking, and now that I have a new knee, I am comfortable walking 10,000 to 12,000 steps a day. But living in Texas with the brutal sun six months out of the year combined with having red hair and fair skin, I have to look for other ways sometimes to get out and about.

Right now, I get up early and walk outside until I get 5000 or so steps. I carry my smart phone with me and an app on the phone counts each step. Then I come back to my apartment, get cooled off and rest a little bit before meeting my friend to drive to a nearby mall. We walk there for a little over 5000 steps where it is air-conditioned and pleasant. I get another thousand or so steps doing housework, walking to the clubhouse to get the mail or running another quick errand around the complex.

For me, the key is to be familiar with where I'm walking when I'm by myself. Because this place is new and a 55+ environment, there are no steps. It's a four-story building built in a rectangle, so I utilize the hallways to rack up the steps on my phone. I know that I'm safe from falling here.

Just as you exercise your body, you need to exercise your brain as well. Did you know that a large percentage of people who contract macular degeneration will suffer depression? What can you do to keep from getting depressed? First of all, talk to your doctor about how you are feeling emotionally. You will be going through some changes, and for some people, change can be really difficult. Things that you like to do either become harder to accomplish or perhaps impossible to do at all. I loved to make handmade quilts and do needlework. I continued to do that for some time. Then it got harder to do and the quality of my work was starting not to be up to my standard. I bought special lamps, special light bulbs, special magnifying help, but eventually, I had to face the fact that I was starting a new phase of my life and some things that I enjoyed in the past I was not going to be able to do any more. It made me sad, but I tried to find other interesting things to do.

If you live in a town large enough to have a university, check with them to see what they might have to offer you.

The University of Texas is about a thirty-minute drive from my apartment complex, and they have an OLLI program there which offers weekly lectures on diverse topics. We attend two lectures in the morning, then have a quick lunch and two more sessions in the afternoon. It is highly enjoyable and gave much fodder for discussions.

Do you enjoy reading? Join a book club. The few big book

stores that are left usually have a few book clubs associated with them. If that's not possible, there are wonderful book clubs online.

I can no longer read a book, but I enjoy getting audible books from the library and listening to them. Books For The Blind is also a wonderful resource, and I have enjoyed their service for several years. They will loan you a machine that looks like a tape recorder, but the books come on a flash drive which you just plug in to the machine. It is easy to use, and one feature that I particularly like is that I can turn the speed up and make it go quite fast. These are wonderful programs, and they are free.

It is important to be with other people. Join the local Kiwanis International Club or the local Rotary Club which are service-oriented organizations. I am sure that you will be greeted warmly at any of their meetings. Another avenue to making friends is the Lions Club. On their website, they say they promote a good environment and good citizenship, but another of its missions is to help blind or low vision children or adults. What could be a better use of your time than helping a child who cannot see?

If none of these suggestions

appeals to you, start something new in your neighborhood or community. Don't isolate yourself.

LET'S TAKE A TRIP

I have always enjoyed traveling. Sometimes I went on a group tour, sometimes with my husband and/or daughter, and sometimes I enjoyed traveling alone. Just because you have decreased vision does not mean that you cannot still get out and about. Let me help you walk through a couple of scenarios.

Let's say that you would like to go to New York City alone. I have gone there several times by myself to attend performances at the Metropolitan Opera at Lincoln center. I felt comfortable for the entire trip because I did some homework before I left home. After you select a date, the next thing to do is to decide where you want to fly. In a large city, you usually have several airports to choose from, so you want to select the closest one to the part of the city you would like to make your home base.

Now you are ready to look for a ticket. Because of my vision problems, I always look at my first option being a flight where I do not have to change planes. After that I look to make sure that the timing is good. I might save a few dollars leaving at 5 a.m., but that just doesn't work for me. When you get your reservation, you will have the opportunity to check whether you are blind or low vision. Be sure to do this; here is why. First of all, your paperwork will come out in large print. Also, the airline representative when you check your luggage will ask you if you need assistance finding your gate. He will call someone to come get you in a wheelchair if you would like. The next reason is when you are waiting at the gate to board, you will be able to get on the plane before First Class does. That will give you extra time to find your seat, stow your carry-on and get settled in your seat without holding up the boarding process. A flight attendant will be there to assist you inside the plane and will help you find your seat if you need them to. If you choose a nonstop option, all you need now to do is exit the plane at the end of your journey. As soon as you get on the walkway leading to the terminal, you will see several wheelchairs lined up, and your name should be on one of them. The person in charge of that chair has your information and will either get you safely and on time to your next flight or will take you to the baggage area. I have always found these men and women helpful. They usually ask if you would like to stop at a restroom or if you would like to pick up something to eat or drink. I believe that they work for the airport and not the airlines. Tipping is not necessary, but they always are glad to get a few extra dollars for their services.

I will have to be honest here. It is a lot less nerve-racking and a lot more fun to travel with a fully sighted friend than by yourself, but I urge you not to miss a wedding in a different time zone because of macular degeneration. And how about a trip to see those grandchildren? They will love it, and so will you. Be independent and live life fully, but do it safely.

But what do you do when something goes wrong on your trip? Let me tell you about an experience that I had going from Indianapolis to Austin to visit my daughter and her family. I was a little worried on the morning of my travel because of the weather. There was snow on the ground, and it was bitterly cold. As I usually do, I gave myself plenty of time to have an Uber driver deliver me to the airport. After checking in and going through security, I settled in with my second cup of coffee. Boarding time came and went, and I was still sitting there. I was not anxious at all since I had a long layover in Atlanta. But after another hour of waiting, I started to squirm a bit. Finally, they announced that we could board. Once I got seated on the plane, I started to relax until the captain said that we needed to have the plane deiced again. "Don't worry," he said assuredly, "it will only take a few minutes." I did a quick calculation to myself and realized I would never make the next flight.

When we landed, I was told to go to an information area, and someone there would help me. It was quite a long line, but when it was my turn, the agent told me that I was going to have to stay all night and come back to the airport the next morning to complete my trip. I told her that I was legally blind and would need extra help. Three young ladies from San Antonio behind me overheard our conversation, and said that they were going on the same flight that I was and offered their assistance.

And thank goodness they did. We had to exit the terminal, and make our way to a queue of buses, each with a small number on them. Without help, I would never have gotten on the right bus. The airline agent had given us vouchers for food for our dinner, but when we got to the hotel, there was not a place to eat or provide room service. Usually, I can feed a family of four at any moment just out of my purse, but not this time. I had absolutely nothing but a breath mint, but I was safe in the hotel and slept reasonably well before getting up at the crack of dawn and heading back to the Atlanta airport.

There are several lessons here. First, always speak up

and ask for help when you need it. Don't act panicky. Just get help. Next, be sure to pack some granola bars or cheese and crackers in your purse or carry-on, and always keep your medications with you for instances such as this.

Now let's talk about packing. Remember the last time you were at the baggage carrousel waiting for your bags? I am sure that you were acutely aware of how many black suitcases came rolling by, so that is why I purchased an outrageously ugly suitcase for my trips. It was the perfect size, for sure, but it was not pretty. Bright orange and aqua chevron stripes set it apart as it made its way with all those sedate black cases. It is true that I was a bit embarrassed from time to time to pick it up and show the world that it was mine, but it served me well. It finally gave up the ghost on the way back to the US from China after sustaining a large gash along its garish side.

Hopefully you will find a suitcase that will be easy to spot, but let's think of some ways that we pack things into that case that will make life easier for you. I have traveled several times to Europe with my church choir. We were singing sometimes eight concerts in ten days, and we wore black pants and a black top. That is a lot of black inside the suitcase when you have macular degeneration. I found it so difficult morning after morning to paw though the dark things to find just what I needed to wear that day. So here is my packing secret given to me by my traveling companion, Liz. The first thing I do is get the trip itinerary and put the day and date on the left side of a piece of paper. Then I put down the activities for the day, and finally I write down what the weather is supposed to be in that location. Then I am ready to assign outfits for each activity every day: travel, rehearsal, performance, sightseeing. And I put each outfit in a plastic bag with a piece of paper on which is written the day and date in LARGE black letters. I also include in the bag any jewelry that I planned to wear with that outfit. I mostly wear black anyway, so I only take black shoes which will go with performance clothes or sightseeing or travel. After the plastic bags and shoes go in the suitcase, I put in underclothing, PJs, etc. I also put adapters and phone chargers in a colorful bag so I always can find them when I need them. Perhaps you can modify this arrangement for yourself of find a game plan that works better for you. The point is, though, be really organized at home while packing your suitcase to prevent frustration while you are supposed to be having a great time.

Handling money has been a problem for me in the past. Many times, I had just put a few bills or coins in my hand and told the sales clerk that I can't see please take the correct amount. Boy, is that Iffy! In a foreign country and in the United States, I do not believe that I was ever cheated. Of course, I was fine buying a slice of pizza or something small. But anything worth more than a few dollars, I used a credit card. Now there are so many apps to put on your phone to help you identify the cash, this is no longer a problem. Be sure to completely familiarize yourself with the app before you leave home.

FINDING HELP

When I was first diagnosed with macular degeneration, the doctor said to me that my biggest problem was going to be making myself ask for help. I think that he could see that I was an independent person. He was right, and I still struggle with this today. But when I was living in Indianapolis, I was watching TV one evening and saw an advertisement that changed my life drastically. It was for an organization called Bosma. The ad said that it was for people who were blind or had low vision. Naturally, it caught my attention, and I quickly called the phone number on the screen.

It was after hours, of course, but I left my name and a short message with my phone number, and a friendly voice from Bosma called me the next day.

Their website, as I learned later, tells us that it is a nonprofit organization that has helped the people in Indiana who have little or no vision. And they have been doing just that over 100 years. I could fill many volumes of books writing about their many programs, but you can go online and read about that yourself. Instead, let me tell you specifically what Bosma did for me.

After the original phone call from them to give and get basic information, a counselor called.

I told her that I had two goals as my disease progressed. One was to be able to stay in my own home, and the other was to remain as independent as possible.

In only a few days, the most wonderful woman, Connie

Michaels, called to make an appointment for a home visit. The first time I met her, I was impressed with her positive attitude and her practical answers to my many questions. This wasn't her first rodeo with macular degeneration! Although about 50% of the people who work for Bosma are either blind or sight-impaired, she seemed to have great vision. She told me that her husband who is blind and had a guide dog was and is vice-president of Bosma.

Over the next few months, and visits from Connie, I learned how to be safe and how NOT to let my life be defined by my failing eyesight. She gave me motivation, courage, and a look into what might be awaiting me as my eyes continued to fail.

Bosma has lots of corporate donors throughout the state, but once a year they have a big bash called DINING IN THE DARK which is held at a large hotel in downtown Indy. It is a black-tie affair, and the attendees are capped at 1,800. I was thrilled, honored, and humbled to be asked to be the keynote speaker one year. After happy hour, dinner was served, but before anyone could take a bite, the MC, Brian Bosma, told us it was time to take out the provided black masks and put them on while we ate our dinner. Everyone was a little stunned how difficult it was to try to do something so simple as eat dinner while not being able to see. I am sure that all of us thought then what a struggle it is for low vision or blind people to do basic things every day. Then it was my turn to tell my story after they showed a beautiful video of all the ways that I had been helped by Bosma. We raised a lot of money, and I was so proud to think that I had a small part in it.

Unfortunately, Bosma is only available to those living in Indiana. I have been unable to find anything even close to it in Texas. I urge you to investigate your state and see what services are available to you. After all, if there are 10 million of us in the United States with this debilitating disease, we should be able to get some assistance.

There are other ways to help. Just the fact that you picked up this book to read shows that you are open to learning more about how to make your life easier and safer. But think of some other things that you can do. Each time I go out to eat, I look at the restaurant's menu on-line before I leave the house and decide then what I will order. Seeing the small print on the menu in a dim restaurant setting is hard for some sighted people to do, much less for a person whose vision is fading.

One of your biggest assets is your smart phone. If you are close to an Apple store, you can sign up for a free Accessibility class and learn how to activate all the low vision helps that are already built into your iPhone. Trust me, you will be amazed. I also have Alexa in my kitchen. She is so helpful to me. She sets times for me, plays the news for me, tells me what time it is and most of all plays beautiful music for me whenever I ask. Her capabilities are practically endless.

I use my iPhone to contact Instacart to order groceries. Yes, I miss going to the grocery store, but this is what I must do at this point in my life. I rarely have even a small a problem with Instacart.

When I moved to the 55+ apartment complex, I felt that it was well-situated so that I could get places easily. What I did not realize is that two of the places that I wanted to go often were across a really busy street, and they were my bank and my drugstore. I could walk to a grocery store, coffee shops, and various other businesses, but not these two essential locations. The street scared me—two lanes each way with two turning lanes. And to make matters worse, the intersection I needed to cross had an equally congested setup. There is a lot of traffic in the area most hours of the day, but I needed to learn to get across that road.

I called the occupational therapist who worked in the office of Dr. Miller, my Low Vision doctor. I was absolutely elated when she told me that she knew someone who specialized in the use of the white cane technique. I had instruction and practice using it while working with specialists at Bosma, but I needed more help getting across the dangerous street.

I made the call to Vivian, the OT, who said that she would be delighted to come help me. She charged me by the hour for five sessions after which I crossed the once perilous intersection by myself thirteen times using my white cane and a lot of pluck!

What an empowerment not to have a barrier between me and where I wanted to go.

YOU CAN DO IT

As I mentioned before, most of you will have a disease that progresses so slowly that you will barely remember that you have it. But for those of you who experience a more severe loss of vision, my hope for you is that you will give yourself permission to TRY. Try to learn new ways to accomplish things.

Try not to be afraid of asking for help. Try to be grateful for the vision that you have rather than lament what has been taken away from you. Try to reach down in the reservoir of strength that each of us has. Tap it as often as needed.

YOU CAN DO THIS.

FINDING JOY EACH DAY

For most of my adult life, I have listened to music by Johann Sebastian Bach each day. It fills me with an intellectual and aesthetic strength. Indeed, it also fills me with spiritual energy and vitality. It is how I find joy each day.

I also love thinking about

my family— my son Jonathan and his wife, Becca, and my granddaughters Elizabeth and Caroline and my grandson Andrew. Even though they live many miles away, I can visit them anytime I want in my mind. They bring me such joy. My daughter Vanessa and her husband Dan live only seven minutes from my apartment. Their children Joseph John (Jack) and my youngest granddaughter Lane give me so much joy.

My special friend John is my sunshine. He makes me happy each hour of the day. I love his comment the other day, "People see us holding hands all the time and they think it's just from affection. Little do they know that we are holding each other up."

I get joy from visiting over the internet and phone with my brother Bob and his wife, Diana, in New Jersey. I am so thankful that he did not inherit this disease as I did.

You need to find your own joy and hold onto it. Thank you for reading this book, and if any part of it helps you, that makes me so happy. Now, go live your life fully. Godspeed.